Careers in
ENGINEERING

A Career in Computer Engineering

A Career in Computer Engineering

Stuart A. Kallen

ReferencePoint Press®

San Diego, CA

© 2019 ReferencePoint Press, Inc.
Printed in the United States

For more information, contact:
ReferencePoint Press, Inc.
PO Box 27779
San Diego, CA 92198
www.ReferencePointPress.com

Picture credits:
cover: bjdlzx/iStockphoto.com
6: Maury Aaseng
11: wavebreakmedia/Shutterstock.com
20: Laura A. Oda/MCT/Newscom
28: dotshock/Shutterstock.com
42: GaudiLab/Shutterstock.com

LIBRARY OF CONGRESS CATALOGING-IN-PUBLICATION DATA

Name: Kallen, Stuart A., 1955, author.
Title: A Career in Computer Engineering/by Stuart A. Kallen.
Description: San Diego, CA: ReferencePoint Press, Inc., 2019. | Series: Careers in Engineering |
    Includes bibliographical references and index. | Audience: Grades 9 to 12.
Identifiers: LCCN 2018021278 (print) | LCCN 2018022000 (ebook) | ISBN 9781682823484 (eBook) |
    ISBN 9781682823477 (hardback)
Subjects: LCSH: Computer engineering—Vocational guidance—Juvenile literature.
Classification: LCC TK7885.5 (ebook) | LCC TK7885.5 .K35 2019 (print) | DDC 621.39023—dc23
LC record available at https://lccn.loc.gov/2018021278

CONTENTS

COMPUTER ENGINEER AT A GLANCE

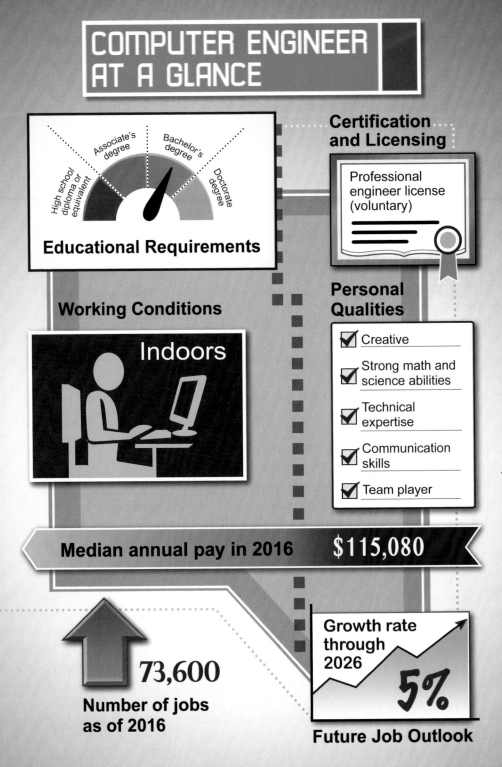

Educational Requirements

High school diploma or equivalent · Associate's degree · Bachelor's degree · Doctorate degree

Certification and Licensing

Professional engineer license (voluntary)

Working Conditions

Indoors

Personal Qualities

- ☑ Creative
- ☑ Strong math and science abilities
- ☑ Technical expertise
- ☑ Communication skills
- ☑ Team player

Median annual pay in 2016 **$115,080**

73,600

Number of jobs as of 2016

Growth rate through 2026 **5%**

Future Job Outlook

Source: Bureau of Labor Statistics, *Occupational Outlook Handbook*. www.bls.gov.

Engineers Make It Work

Every day countless people dream of founding a successful technology company like Apple or Microsoft. These visionaries might go as far to imagine a company founded on a game-changing product and even pencil out the money they hope to make from their unique idea. But every tech dreamer who would like to start a company would do well to follow the advice of Apple cofounder Steve Wozniak: "We have ideas for companies, ideas for revenues and products. [But] don't forget to include the engineers—they are trained to solve problems. That's what they're really good at."[1] There are few careers as versatile as engineering, and engineers rely on multiple talents and skills to solve problems. Engineers use their knowledge of math, science, analysis, and design—and even art—to produce new machines, materials, systems, and structures. They spend their days identifying problems to solve, proposing various solutions, testing concepts, and investigating data.

Wozniak, affectionately known as Woz, is a computer scientist and electrical engineer. He invented the first Apple computers that launched the personal computing revolution in the late 1970s. Wozniak understands that a clever idea or a new approach to marketing a product is not enough to achieve success. Engineers are needed to turn an idea into reality: "Does it work? For engineering, everything has to work."[2] says Wozniak.

An Exciting and Promising Field

Perhaps no specialty has transformed society more profoundly than computer engineering, which is a subdiscipline of electrical engineering. Computers have changed the way people communicate, learn, shop, travel, play games, make music, watch movies, and even exercise. And computer engineers are the masterminds behind the digital revolution. These professionals design, test, construct, and maintain computers and computer-controlled equipment.

The work of computer engineers can be seen in laptop, desktop, and tablet computers. Computer engineers also design workstations, printers, modems, network servers, smartphones, and supercomputers. In addition they are creators of the internal hardware elements that make computers function smoothly and efficiently. These components include motherboards, memory chips, processors, video cards, hard drives, and power supplies. Computer engineers embed computers in cars, airplanes, appliances, and other machines. They build hardware for communications networks and labor to make computers faster, smaller, and smarter.

> "The opportunity to have an original impact through building important and specialized [computers] is larger than anything I've seen before."[3]
>
> —MIT engineering professor Joel Emer

The work of computer engineers produces industrial computer systems used for manufacturing, energy production, agriculture, and other businesses. If a device has any digital functions, a computer hardware engineer helped design and test it. The work also requires computer engineers to have a thorough knowledge of computer software, and most are experts at writing computer code. They work with operating systems, applications, utilities, and security programs.

Computer engineers who focus on the future are working to incorporate digital functions into fabrics and building materials. Some are building hardware for the next generation of artificial intelligence, creating powerful computer hardware for driverless cars, drones, and spacecraft. Massachusetts Institute of Technology (MIT) professor Joel Emer is thrilled about the future of computer engineering: "I've been in this field for more than four decades. I've never seen an area with so much excitement and promise in all that time. The opportunity to have an original impact through building important and specialized [computer] architecture is larger than anything I've seen before."[3]

"Build Good Computers"

Most computer engineers work behind the scenes to innovate and create new products. But a few computer science pioneers went on to become well-known tech luminaries. Jeff Bezos trained as a computer engineer before starting the online retail site Amazon .com. Facebook cofounder Dustin Moskovitz, Twitter cofounder Jack Dorsey, and superstar computer games developer Markus Persson all began their careers as computer engineers.

And of course there is Woz, who as a teenager had a poster of a 1970s Cray supercomputer pinned on the wall of his bedroom. Like many pioneers, Wozniak's genius was not immediately recognized; his design for the Apple I computer was turned down by Hewlett-Packard on five occasions. Woz went on to found Apple with Steve Jobs who transformed the world with iPods, iPads, and iPhones. But unlike Jobs, Woz had no desire to conquer the tech world. As he stated in 2006, "My goal wasn't to make a ton of money. It was to build good computers. I only started the company when I realized I could be an engineer forever."[4] For those who dream of engineering computers forever, the field is practically unlimited during an era where computers are harvesting food, driving cars, and guiding rockets to Mars and beyond.

CHAPTER 1

What Does a Computer Engineer Do?

Computer engineers work with extremely complex equipment, and their job description can be equally complicated. Computer engineers apply their knowledge of electronics to computer hardware, computer systems engineering, and computer architecture (the basic construction and low-level programming of computers). Hardware engineers specialize in researching, developing, designing, and testing computer equipment that can range from pocket calculators to the giant servers used by social media and video streaming websites. Some invent and develop new equipment, while others update computers to make them faster and more efficient.

Computer systems engineers develop, test, and evaluate systems made up of computer circuits, microchips, and computer hardware components. They design internal hardware components, including data processors, graphics processing units (GPUs), and the central processing units (CPUs) that execute most of the commands from a computer's hardware and software. Computer engineer Dave Haynie explains his job: "I do system-level design . . . which means working out systems based on chips. . . . There are plenty of computer engineers who only design parts of very large systems, but I actually design whole computer systems."[5]

Other whole computer systems include information technology (IT) networks used by businesses and other organizations. Computer engineers who work in IT develop and manage systems made up of integrated components that manage operations, process financial accounts, control human resource information, and deliver digital products like e-books, music, movies, and games.

Computer engineers work in a variety of areas including hardware, systems engineering, and computer architecture. They might work with giant servers (pictured), tiny microchips, or other devices and technologies that enable computers to function.

While systems engineers work to create digital structures, other computer engineers focus on designing single chips, or even small parts of a chip. As Haynie says: "A buddy of mine . . . designed the DDR3 memory controller on the X-Box 360. That's a piece of a chip, of course, but a very critical one."[6]

Computer Engineering and Computer Science

The field of computer engineering significantly overlaps with that of computer science. Professionals in both fields understand the inner workings of computers and the software aspects of computer systems. What makes computer science unique is that the discipline originated in the 1970s at university math departments, whereas computer engineering grew out of electrical engineering departments. As a result computer science focuses on programming, computation, and algorithms (precise, step-by-step instructions that form the basis of computer programs). The difference between computer science and computer engineering is a matter of emphasis. Computer scientists work in theory and experimentation, while computer engineers are more likely to design, test, and build hardware.

Since computer engineers work with operating systems and software applications, they are experts in hardware-software integration. The smartphone industry provides a good example of this integration; new hardware and software is introduced simultaneously. This requires computer engineers to write, test, and analyze the software that will run on the devices they design. In this role computer engineers might develop software apps used for word processing, spreadsheets, database management, networking, utilities, and security. Computer engineers also write firmware, the computer programs that permanently control specific hardware in a device.

Computers Everywhere

The hardware components developed by computer engineers are used for information processing, communications, and storage. Products invented and produced by computer engineers can be found in a wide range of industries, including telecommunications, robotics, energy, health care, security, entertainment, gaming, and manufacturing.

Computer engineers are also behind the wide range of "smart" devices available to consumers. These gadgets, which include televisions, fitness trackers, refrigerators, home security systems, and even coffeepots, are embedded with complete computers built onto a single circuit board known as single board computers (SBCs). These small computing devices communicate to one another on a giant digital network called the Internet of Things (IoT) that is expected to drive the economy of the future. According to the research center McKinsey Global Institute, the IoT could be worth between $3.9 trillion and $11.1 trillion by 2025. By that time over 35 billion devices will be connected to the IoT. And computer engineers will be central to this development, as tech writer Daniel Burrus explains: "The Internet of Things revolves around increased machine-to-machine communication; it's built on cloud computing and networks of data-gathering sensors; it's mobile, virtual, and [allows] instantaneous connection."[7]

Some computer engineers work in the automotive field designing vehicles that can be described as computers on wheels. Every new car rolling off an assembly line has up to 150 embedded computer-controlled devices. Computer engineers design and test switches, sensors, drivers, microcontrollers, and other components in charge of everything from adjusting seats to regulating gas flow into the engine. Autonomous (self-driving) cars use even more complex digital systems. As automobile companies rush to develop autonomous cars, computer engineers are in great demand, according to computer engineer Sebastian Thrun: "It's not just the physical car but areas like navigation, LiDAR [long-range radar], cameras . . . so the need for [computer engineering] talent, both in hardware and software, is huge."[8]

> "It's not just the physical car but areas like navigation, LiDAR, cameras . . . so the need for [computer engineering] talent, both in hardware and software, is huge."[8]
>
> —Sebastian Thrun, computer engineer

Beyond typical consumer products, computer engineers design, test, and build industrial equipment in a field called computer-aided manufacturing (CAM). Those who work in CAM combine software with machinery that is used to automate manufacturing processes. CAM systems control all operations at a manufacturing plant, including production, transportation, management, and storage. Computers are central to CAM, which reduces waste, saves energy, increases production speeds, creates more consistent products, and efficiently tracks and orders materials. Industrial robots rely on embedded computers that program actions such as moving parts and materials, assembling products, and performing precise operations that are difficult or impossible for

Computers in Space

Outer space might be one of the most exciting new environments for computer engineering. In 2018 computer engineers at the University of Pittsburgh's NSF Center for Space, High-performance, and Resilient Computing (SHREC) launched one of the world's most powerful computers into orbit. The Space Test Program-Houston 6 (STP-H6) is a supercomputer built for the International Space Station (ISS), and it is three times more powerful than its predecessor. Computer engineers designed the STP-H6 with special shielding that allows the supercomputer to withstand galactic cosmic rays and other types of radiation found in the extreme environment of outer space. The computer will be used to perform numerous experiments while taking detailed pictures of Earth with its dual high-resolution cameras. SHREC founder Alan George explains: "Computer engineering for space is the ultimate challenge . . . since remote sensing [the scanning of the earth by satellite] and autonomous operation are the main purposes of spacecraft and both demand high-performance computing."

Quoted in Matt Cichowicz, "Engineering Team Develops Radiation-Resistant Computers Capable of High-Performance Computing in the Harshness of Space," Phys.org, March 6, 2018. https://phys.org.

humans. For example, robots are used at auto assembly plants to lift heavy car bodies and move them from one assembly line to another. Robots stamp out metal pieces, perform welding tasks, and operate paint sprayers. They can also perform delicate tasks like embedding computer chips in dashboards.

Rethink Robotics in Boston built a robot named Sawyer to fabricate metal, assemble circuit boards, and load and unload parts. Rethink Robotics vice president Matt Fitzgerald describes Sawyer as a big bundle of sensors: "Sawyer has an embedded camera in the robot for locating parts before picking or placing. You can track . . . how much force was used when placing something into a fixture. It can tell you the run-time hours and the parts count."[9]

Artificial Intelligence

Industrial robots are evolving rapidly as computer engineers develop next-gen machines that are autonomous. These robots run on artificial intelligence (AI), computer "brains" that can reason and learn. AI computers rely on automatic code generation; the machines can adjust, produce, or change their programming depending on the situation. A good example of this machine learning can be seen in the Tesla Model S electric car, which can drive semi-autonomously. The autopilot feature on the Tesla allows the car to collect millions of miles of driving data from its human drivers. Sensors pick up information about acceleration, braking, and even driver hand placement on the steering wheel and other controls. Instead of programming the car to drive autonomously, the car learns on its own by observing human drivers. As Tesla chief executive officer (CEO) and computer engineer Elon Musk explains, each driver becomes "an expert trainer."[10] The cars also communicate with one another over the Tesla network to share the driving knowledge they pick up from their expert trainers. The information is used to create what are called data maps that contain the average speed, traffic patterns, and hazards found on specific stretches of highway. This information is transmitted to any Tesla that travels on the road and helps the car better navigate stop-and-go traffic, rain, snow, and other conditions.

> "Many [artificial intelligence] accomplishments were made possible because of advances in hardware. Hardware is the foundation of everything you can do."[12]
>
> —MIT engineering professor Joel Emer

In 2018 the field of artificial intelligence was still in its infancy. As language expert Erik Cambria notes, "There is [no machine] today that is even barely as intelligent as the most stupid human being on Earth."[11] But the field is rapidly advancing, and computer engineers are designing the instruments necessary to create the AI systems of the future. As MIT professor Joel Emer points out: "The value of the hardware at the heart of [AI] is often overlooked. . . . Many AI accomplishments were made possible because of advances in hardware. Hardware is the foundation of everything you can do in software."[12]

Quantum Computing

Perhaps the most advanced work performed by computer engineers is taking place in the field of quantum computing. Quantum computers function much differently than digital computers. Conventional computers process data encoded in binary digits, or bits. Each bit can only be defined as one or zero. Quantum computers work with quantum bits, or qubits, that exist on an atomic level. Qubits can exist in multiple states, which allow them to transmit information many times faster than binary digital computers. As might be expected, the science behind quantum computing is extremely complex. Single phosphorus atoms embedded in silicon can become entangled with one another to produce what are called logical qubits. These particles can theoretically communicate with one another. A computer using just three hundred logical qubits would possess more computing power than all the world's conventional computers connected together.

The field of medicine is expected to provide one of the main applications for quantum computers. Qubits could be used to rapidly sequence a patient's genes in seconds and evaluate all the possible interactions between molecules, proteins, and chemicals. This would allow for personalized drug treatment.

The Brain-Computer Interface

Quantum computing is at the heart of Musk's 2017 venture called Neuralink. The company is working to develop what Musk calls a brain-computer interface. Such devices could theoretically be implanted in the brain to help humans merge with computer software programs. Musk believes that humans will need a brain-computer interface in the future to communicate directly with machines while keeping pace with artificial intelligence.

Musk notes that some computers communicate at a rate of a trillion bits per second, while a human typing on a smartphone is limited to ten bits per second. He believes that tiny, implantable computers need to be created so that humans and machines can achieve some sort of balance. As Musk told an audience at the World Government Summit in Dubai in 2017: "Over time I think we will probably see a closer merger of biological intelligence and digital intelligence. It's mostly about the bandwidth, the speed of the connection between your brain and the digital version of yourself."[13]

Computer engineers will continue to be at the forefront of those who design and build the fastest, smartest, and smallest machines ever created. And today's computer engineering miracles will be overshadowed by the cutting-edge inventions of tomorrow. From satellites circling the earth to the atomic particles surging through the brain, computer engineers are the pioneers leading a digital revolution that continues to transform society and culture in ways simple and profound.

CHAPTER 2

How Do You Become a Computer Engineer?

A bachelor of science degree in computer engineering or a related subject is required by all employers that produce computer hardware. And students wishing to become computer engineers need to become proficient in many complex subjects. While this might feel overwhelming, prospective computer engineers can get a head start on their careers by making high school count.

Many of the courses needed for a computer science degree can be first taken in high school. For example, math is the foundation for all computer science, and students should take as many math courses as possible. As Google software engineer Eric Willisson explains, "Math classes are good because they help you learn to think in the logical ways that help with computers. Algebra is useful for understanding many algorithms later, geometry helps if you're going to do any graphics and can help with graph theory (which, again, helps with many algorithms), and I have always found calculus showing up in unexpected places."[14]

> "Math classes are good because they help you learn to think in the logical ways that help with computers."[14]
>
> —Eric Willisson, software engineer

Any technology using electricity, mechanics, heat, light, sound, and optics is based on physics. Since computers use all of the above, prospective computer engineers should add physics classes to their high school curriculum. The courses teach about how things work while breaking them down into smaller and smaller components to see how each bit functions independently. Computer engineering is almost entirely applied physics, and the study of physics will help prospective computer engineers grasp how circuits, processors, and other components function.

Tech Camps

Prospective computer engineering students can get a jump-start on college by attending tech summer camps. These camps, designed for future computer engineers, coders, and other tech lovers, provide a great way for students to learn while they have fun. Weeklong summer iD Tech Camps are offered at more than eighty prestigious universities in thirty states from coast to coast. Summer iD Tech Camps are also available to students in Hong Kong, Singapore, and the United Kingdom. Cutting-edge programs are tailored to various age groups from seven through seventeen. High school students can learn to code apps and games, create and code wearable tech, build robots, and study artificial intelligence and machine learning.

The Digital Media Academy is another summer camp that spotlights STEM (science, technology, engineering, and math) subjects. The academy was founded in 2002, and since that time over 155,000 students have learned and lived at college campuses in the United States and Canada, including Northwestern, Duke, University of Washington, and University of Toronto. Campers study programming, robotics, engineering, and other topics of interest to future computer engineers.

Beyond science, prospective computer engineers need to be able to write well and communicate clearly. High school students should not neglect English classes, as Willisson explains: "Programmers who document their code well are few, far between, and highly valuable."[15] In addition many computer professionals found that classes in art, philosophy, history, and music helped them solve problems by thinking more creatively. According to an unnamed source quoted in the *Princeton Review*: "One of the biggest surprises in my 25 years of technology work is that people who have a creative background . . . [tend to] see and grasp big-picture concepts very quickly, and break them down into sub-components. People who [only] have a computer engineering or math background tend to be very technical, and sometimes that can be a hindrance."[16]

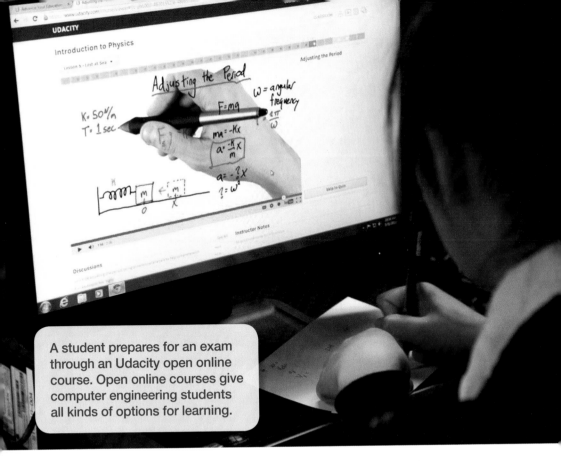

A student prepares for an exam through an Udacity open online course. Open online courses give computer engineering students all kinds of options for learning.

Massive Open Online Courses

Every computer engineer needs strong programming skills so that writing code becomes second nature. High school students should be familiar with programming languages such as AngularJS, Python, JavaScript, Ruby, and C++. High school students, college students, and anyone else who wants to learn to code or improve their programming skills can visit the website Codecademy. The site is categorized as a Massive Open Online Course, or MOOC. These open online courses offer access to classes on the web with unlimited participation. Codecademy provides free interactive coding classes in twelve different programming languages. For around twenty dollars a month, coders can sign up for "Pro" classes, which offer more personalized training.

The web offers numerous other free or inexpensive MOOCs that can help prepare high school students for a career in computer engineering. Over 29 million people have registered to take classes at Coursera, which hosts over two thousand courses from top-rated colleges and universities, including Stanford, Yale, and Princeton. The site features courses in algorithms, artificial intelligence, programming languages, machine learning, and other subjects of interest for future computer engineers. Some of the online courses might be too advanced for the average high school student. However, the classes can shine a light on the world of computer engineering while providing inexpensive guidance. As computer engineering and Coursera student Feynman Liang explains, "I get to gain a nontrivial understanding of a field. And it translates into me doing a lot better in college. . . . You really don't need a certificate or official recognition for what you take away from the classes [for them] to be useful to you."[17]

Several other popular MOOCs offer classes aimed at prospective computer engineers. The edX website, which provides free courses from Harvard, MIT, and nearly one hundred other institutions, emphasizes computer science, programming, and computer engineering. Udacity, which is sponsored by Amazon, Google, IBM, and other tech companies, offers courses in virtual reality development, engineering self-driving cars, and robotic engineering.

Precollege Summer School

High school students who prefer classroom learning over online courses can prep for a bachelor of science degree by attending summer school at colleges and universities. Summer school, referred to as precollege summer programs, offers high school students opportunities to expand their knowledge. Participants might also make valuable connections with professors who can write letters of recommendation to include with college applications.

While hundreds of colleges offer summer precollege programs, the University of California (UC) system is ranked among the best. Open to students in grades nine through twelve, the UC Summer School for Mathematics and Science is a four-week residential program. Topics extend beyond typical curricula found in high schools, with a strong emphasis on science, technology, and computer engineering. Several courses are of interest to prospective computer engineers. Robot Inventors offers students the opportunity to build their own robots. Another course called Engineering Design and Control of Kinetic Sculptures focuses on utilizing microprocessors, microcontrollers, and other hardware to build sculptures that climb, bounce, fall, and perform other movements.

Stanford University is working to increase diversity in the computer engineering field with its Artificial Intelligence Laboratory's Outreach Summer Program. The course is open to girls who are interested in exploring hardware and software used for AI applications. The two-week class provides faculty lectures, field trips, hands-on projects, and mentoring sessions.

Cornell University in Ithaca, New York, is a top-rated engineering school and offers the Cornell Engineering Experience, a six-week residential summer program. The courses focus on math, computer science, and physics. Precollege students combine lab work with cutting-edge research and are able to meet with the college's engineering professors and representatives from its admissions office.

Other top-rated precollege programs include Harvard University's Secondary School Program, Johns Hopkins University's Engineering Innovation, and the Computational Science Class for High School Students at Illinois Tech in Chicago. The Game Lab Summer Institute at University of California, Los Angeles (UCLA) is perhaps the most unique precollege summer technology program. The two-week course offers instruction in video and mobile games and gaming hardware.

Obtain a Bachelor's Degree

Completion of a precollege summer program provides a great addition to a college application, but it is not mandatory. High school students wishing to enroll in a computer engineering degree program should choose a school that is certified by the Accreditation Board for Engineering and Technology (ABET). This organization provides assurance that programs meet the quality standards of the engineering profession. In 2018 ABET accredited over 3,800 programs at 770 colleges and universities in thirty-one countries.

Coursework for a four-year bachelor's degree in computer engineering covers subjects specific to the field. Core computer engineering classes include introduction to software engineering, computer programming, computer architecture, applied algorithms for engineering, microprocessors, electrical design, signal processing, logic design, and mathematical structures related to computer hardware and software. Other coursework covers scientific subjects such as physics and chemistry.

While the coursework may sound dizzying, the lab work can be fun, according to Nishil Shah, a computer engineering student at the University of Texas:

> I got to take an advanced embedded systems lab course where my group chose to build a Bluetooth music player as our final project. We did all of the circuit and [circuit board] work like integrating the speakers, the processor, resistors, the Bluetooth module, an SD card, the LCD screen, and much more. We also wrote the software so you could select which song to play and how to store a song on the SD card that was being downloaded via Bluetooth.[18]

Benefits of a Graduate Degree

Many good jobs are available for those with bachelor's degrees in computer engineering. But according to a 2017 study by the job information organization CareerOneStop, 26 percent of computer engineers hold a master's degree. These professionals obtain the best positions and highest salaries, and they oversee the most interesting projects.

Students pursuing a master of science in computer engineering spend their first year completing course requirements that emphasize cybersecurity, computer connections and networks, and computer hardware architecture. Second-year students pursue specific areas of interest, often in computer science or electrical engineering. Other classes include systems engineering, computer systems security foundations, probability for computer and electrical engineers, broadband network architectures, and modern active circuit design. Most master's programs incorporate what are called capstone projects in the final year. A capstone

Work as an Intern

Whatever a computer engineer's educational background might be, an internship will provide some of the vital experience that managers look for on a résumé. Internships provide hands-on development experience and knowledge of hardware and software systems. Those who work as interns often find mentors who help them learn. Florida International University computer engineering student Alastair Paragas describes the benefits of his internship at CERN, home of the hadron collider in Geneva, Switzerland: "[I was able to] network with highly intelligent people coming from diverse fields of study, ranging from physics, mathematics, mechanical engineering and computer science. I am always humbled working with behemoths from their respective fields, living and working on the shoulders of giants."

Professors often link students to internships, but positions can be obtained by e-mailing the numerous tech companies that offer summer intern positions. Candidates work with teams in a fast-moving environment to integrate, deploy, and support complex computer systems. Interns participate in research and development, problem-solving, maintenance, and other tasks. To qualify for internships, candidates are required to be enrolled in a college or university, and they must be familiar with various computer hardware, operating systems, and coding.

Quoted in Millie Acebal, "My Internship with CERN," FIU News, May 15, 2017. https://news.fiu.edu.

project is a question or problem that students choose and pursue independent research on the subject.

Those who wish to teach at the university level or conduct computer engineering research need to obtain a doctorate (PhD), which requires a four- to seven-year commitment. This process requires students to be accepted into a program, complete course work, and write a lengthy research-based essay called a dissertation. Pinterest product engineer Tracy Chou describes how participating in a PhD program helped her personal growth:

You pick up research and critical thinking skills. You learn to think independently. . . . You learn how to break down problems, and set about seeking to solve them. You learn to be self-motivated, because a PhD program is so free-form that you'll have to set your own schedule and dead-lines. You get to spend a few years thinking deeply about a problem that you're interested in . . . without the pressure of a boss who needs something for a product deadline or a company that needs to hit revenue targets or other such external constraints.[19]

Chou lists disadvantages as well. Holders of PhDs are over-qualified for many computer industry jobs, which means they might only be able to initially find work as coders. This would make it difficult to defray the added costs of obtaining a doctorate degree. Additionally, employers often view doctoral candidates, who spent years in academic settings, as out of touch with the latest advances in industry. And most start-ups cannot afford to hire PhDs. But, according to Chou, the advantages of obtaining a PhD outweigh the disadvantages: "Some of the more prestigious director or VP roles are reserved for people who have PhDs, especially if they are to oversee very technical areas. [And] if you get very, very lucky, you can start a company to commercialize your research in a field with a high barrier to entry because of the technical depth."[20]

Get Certified

Certification is not required for a career in computer engineering. However, certification serves as a badge of approval, and those who hold official credentials can expect higher wages. The Institute of Electrical and Electronics Engineers (IEEE) is the primary organization that provides software certification for computer engineers. The IEEE awards various certifications to those who complete an extensive two-part online exam. A passing score qualifies an individual as a Certified Software Development Professional (CSDP).

Other certifications are awarded by vendors to those who specialize in their systems. Cisco, which builds networking hardware and other high-tech equipment, offers a certification ladder. It starts on lower rungs and moves up to more complex certifications. For example, the Cisco Certified Design Associate (CCDA) and Cisco Certified Design Professional (CCDP) certifications can lead to jobs in computer networking architecture. Computer engineers can continue to climb up the certification ladder by obtaining the Cisco Certified Design Expert (CCDE), which is a prerequisite for the Cisco Certified Architect (CCAr). At this level a computer engineer can also obtain certifications in Cisco Certified Internetwork Expert (CCIE), Routing and Switching or Data Center.

"You will have to constantly learn. You need to be very much aware of not just the technologies available today but about the trends."[21]

—Peter Steenkiste, professor of computer engineering

Obtaining certification is part of the lifelong learning process associated with the computer engineering profession. Computer engineers constantly update their knowledge. They read books and journals, attend conferences, and take classes to stay informed about the latest changes in technology. As professor of computer engineering at Carnegie Mellon University Peter Steenkiste explains, "You will have to constantly learn. You need to be very much aware of not just the technologies available today but about the trends."[21]

It takes great dedication to earn a degree in computer engineering, but it is not all hard work. And many students who major in computer engineering say they love the hands-on projects, the teamwork, the design competitions, and other features of the program. The classes can make science and math lively and interesting, and a degree in computer engineering is a ticket to an exciting career marked by good pay, fascinating work, and next-gen research.

What Skills and Personal Qualities Matter Most— and Why?

Engineers are highly respected professionals, but they often battle common misconceptions about their vocation. Engineers are often painted as introverted, math-loving nerds who lack creative skills. Mechanical engineer Brandon R. Buckhalt founded the Creative Engineer website to dispel the stereotypes: "Engineers are the builders, the believers, the inventors, the creative geniuses, and the optimistic go-getters that have guided our civilization out of the caves and onto the moon."[22]

The term *engineer* comes from the Latin word for ingenuity, *ingeniator*. And engineers have historically been viewed as inventive people, those who use ingenuity and creative thought processes to solve problems. At the same time, engineering requires a great deal of personal discipline since the highly technical work can be brutally difficult. Buckhalt's wife, Lisa, is also an engineer, and she offers her summation of the work: "Engineering requires the fortitude to enthusiastically apply your energy toward a task you find undesirable."[23]

> "Engineers are the builders, the believers, the inventors, the creative geniuses, and the optimistic go-getters that have guided our civilization out of the caves and onto the moon."[22]
>
> —Brandon R. Buckhalt, mechanical engineer

Enthusiastically applying energy to difficult tasks requires skills that fit into three broad categories. Computer engineers rely on technical skills, operational skills, and what might be called character skills. Education forms the basis for technical skills that

Computer engineers typically work in teams. This requires solid communication skills as well as the ability to cooperate with colleagues who might be working hundreds or thousands of miles away.

computer engineers use to analyze and understand problems. Internships and job experience provide operational skills that computer engineers rely on to perform experiments and complete tasks. Character skills are those that help computer engineers work well with others. They include self-motivation, determination, passion for the work, good communication abilities, and the capacity to work seamlessly as a team player.

Technical Skills

Technical skills are also called *hard skills*, a term that can have two meanings. Hard skills provide a rock-solid basis of knowledge required for computer engineering. Hard skills are also hard to master. That is why some students of computer architecture refer to the classes as "computer archi-torture." Joking aside, the job of a computer engineer is to utilize hard skills like science, technology, engineering, and math to design systems, run tests, and invent solutions to problems. Technical knowledge includes a good understanding of circuit boards, processors, chips, computer hardware and software, networking equipment, and other electronics.

While computer engineers are not necessarily "mathletes," they do rely on a strong understanding of mathematics to invent systems, components, and processes. Computer engineers use differential equations and linear algebra when working with circuits. And they use math skills to create algorithms. As computer engineer Naman Attri writes, "If you know how to build algorithms, learning any programming language becomes a piece of cake."[24]

While computer programs can be used to solve mathematical problems, computer engineers still need razor-sharp math skills. As engineering career counselor Alison Doyle explains, "The existence of computers does not free you from the need to understand math. In fact, since computers can only follow instructions, engineers must first figure out how to solve numeric problems on their own before they can tell a computer what to do."[25]

While computer engineers create their own programs and apps, they also work with computer modeling software, which is used to create complex systems and conduct experiments to ensure the systems work. Computer modeling methodology is used to design components and observe them from different points of view. Computer engineers also rely on modeling programs to produce techniques for building hardware.

Computer engineers draw on their analytical skills to identify the strengths and weaknesses of experiments. They use impartial analysis to evaluate the technical solutions that result from the experimentation. A talent for logic and reasoning helps computer engineers find solutions that function within the framework of budgets, production schedules, and other business concerns.

Operational Skills

As the name implies, operational skills help computer engineers operate efficiently on a day-to-day basis. Attention to detail is an operational skill especially important in the computer engineering field. Computer engineers work with intricate parts, such as circuits and processors, and search for the tiniest bugs and glitches in computer programs. These professionals must not only have an eye for detail when examining physical structures or lines of code, but they also need to be patient and persistent when solving problems.

Problem-solving and critical-thinking skills work together to help a computer engineer identify a problem and evaluate solutions to find the proper remedy. Multitasking skills are important for computer engineers who need to remain organized and focused while simultaneously dealing with puzzling plans, tiny pieces of hardware, and demands from production managers and CEOs.

Computer engineers need to be good readers who can learn from manuals, technical journals, and periodicals. Reading helps engineers identify new design tools, implement recent technology, and keep up with changes in the industry. Computer engineers also need to be adept at technical writing to describe complex concepts in a clear, concise manner. Computer engineers are often called upon to write memos and instruct less technically inclined employees on numerous issues from implementing new algorithms to using recently developed equipment.

> "I have met very few engineers who are comfortable with using simple language, organizing documents for the readers' benefit, keeping sentences and paragraphs short, and getting to the point."[26]
>
> —Gary Blake, technical writing instructor

Computer engineers also write scientific papers for technical periodicals and for presentations at conferences. Beyond technical subjects, most computer engineers are expected to write trip reports, business proposals, and reports on lab experiments. This operational skill, while particularly important, is a rarity in the computer engineering field, as technical writing instructor Gary Blake points out: "In my 25 years of teaching seminars in technical writing, I have met very few engineers who are comfortable with using simple language, organizing documents for the readers' benefit, keeping sentences and paragraphs short, and getting to the point."[26]

This advice carries over to conversation. Computer engineers sometimes need to be reminded to speak in sentences rather than long-winded paragraphs. They need to translate the technical language of computer engineering into plain English for multiple stakeholders in a project, which might include bosses, assistants, marketing executives, and customers. As executive coach Stacey Hanke explains, people are bombarded with messages all day: "Speaking in short bullet point sentences, pausing to allow your listeners to stay with you will help you be heard above the noise."[27]

Character Skills

Character skills are sometimes referred to as soft skills, which generally refer to the capacity to work well with others. An engineering blogger known as 3DX explains: "Nobody completes an engineering project by themselves: there is a vast team working on various parts of the project."[28] This means computer engineers must work well with groups that might include members from culturally diverse research teams, global corporations, and experts from other scientific disciplines. Workplace expert Amy Cooper Hakim explains that character skills cannot be learned in a classroom: "[A computer engineer] can be taught how to use a certain computer program much more quickly than she can be taught how to establish rapport or trust with a colleague or customer. Bosses look for those with excellent [character] skills to lead others, to gain customers and to share and promote ideas in group settings."[29]

While character skills come naturally to some, others need to make an effort to perfect them. Job counselors say interactions with others are made easier by making eye contact. Looking into a person's eyes helps establish trust, and as economist Joseph Stiglitz wrote in 2013, "It's trust, more than money, that makes the world go round."[30] This is especially true for computer engineers who are seeking employment. According to a poll by the job recruiting website iCims, 68 percent of job recruiters say the most common mistake job applicants make is avoiding eye contact.

Establishing trust is also important for computer engineers who work as team leaders. Coworkers listen better when trust is established, and they will take risks if they know they will be supported if projects do not go as planned. Team leaders also rely on character skills to motivate others. They provide clear guidance

Hard Skills and Soft Skills

In past decades employers were mostly interested in job applicants who possessed hard skills, the technical engineering abilities necessary to perform specific tasks. However, in recent years job recruiters are placing much more importance on soft skills that include communication, professionalism, and enthusiasm. Career expert Alison Doyle delves into the differences between hard and soft skills:

> Hard skills are teachable abilities or skill sets that are easy to quantify. Typically, you'll learn hard skills in the classroom, through books or other training materials, or on the job. . . . Soft skills, on the other hand, are subjective skills that are much harder to quantify. Also known as "people skills" or "interpersonal skills," soft skills relate to the way you relate to and interact with other people. Examples of soft skills include communication, flexibility, leadership, motivation, patience . . . problem solving abilities, teamwork, time management, [and] work ethic.
>
> While certain hard skills are necessary for any position, employers increasingly look for job applicants with particular soft skills. This is because, while it is easy for an employer to train a new employee in a particular hard skill (such as how to use a certain computer program), it is much more difficult to train an employee in a soft skill (such as patience).

Alison Doyle, "Hard Skills vs. Soft Skills: What's the Difference?," Balance Careers, March 21, 2018. www .thebalance.com.

and direction and willingly listen to others. They know when to step in to help struggling coworkers and when to back off.

Leaders need to understand how to utilize the strengths of others while setting realistic goals. They do not create schedules or develop plans that are too ambitious. Additionally, leaders must have high ethical standards and a strong sense of professionalism.

They use resources in a wise and prudent manner and keep everyone informed about a project's progress and problems.

Successful computer engineers need to be open-minded and willing to change plans and adapt to new conditions when unforeseen problems arise. This mind-set requires computer engineers to see the big picture and concentrate on the outcome while overlooking small problems and immediate concerns. This type of focus helps computer engineers plan for any conceivable problems that might arise. They have contingency procedures in place when the unexpected happens. A focus on the big picture also allows computer engineering professionals to take advantage of opportunities, such as the introduction of a new technology or a novel way of completing a project with more efficiency at a lower cost.

The desire to self-educate throughout a career is another character skill used by computer engineers. Continuous learning is necessary since technology changes rapidly; more than half of everything a computer engineer knows today will be obsolete in a few years.

Strengths and Weaknesses

Computer engineering is considered one of the most difficult disciplines to master. But well-honed technical, operational, and character skills make life easier for those who work in the computer engineering field. While most engineers do not possess every necessary skill and personality trait, they all bring different strengths and weaknesses to the job. And all computer engineers have essential skills in common, which has allowed them to collectively design, test, produce, and market the computerized infrastructure that runs the modern world.

While students contemplating a career in computer engineering might be intimidated by the skills of top computer engineers, they have the luxury of developing and refining the traits over time. All that is needed is a focus on the future and a strong desire for self-improvement. With some ingenuity and experience, prospective computer engineers will be able to thrive in a career that is at the cutting edge of the digital revolution.

What Is It like to Work as a Computer Engineer?

The iPhone might be one of the most stunning achievements in computer engineering in recent decades, and computer engineers still dream of working for Apple where the smartphone was invented. The story behind the development of the iPhone reveals a great deal about work life at the world's most profitable company.

When work began on the iPhone in 2005, the computer engineers who were recruited to develop the project were sworn to secrecy. They were also told that their lives would permanently change. Project manager and engineer Scott Forstall describes how he recruited the engineers from within the ranks at Apple: "We're starting a new project," Forstall told them. "It's so secret, I can't even tell you what that new project is. I cannot tell you who you will work for. What I can tell you is if you choose to accept this role, you're going to work harder than you ever have in your entire life. You're going to have to give up nights and weekends probably for a couple years as we make this product."[31]

The CIA Triad

What Apple computer engineers were asked to observe was a set of rules that tech companies often adhere to when developing new products. The rules have the ominous-sounding name "CIA triad" but have nothing to do with the Central Intelligence Agency. The acronym stands for confidentiality, integrity, and availability. In this context, confidentiality describes measures put into place to prevent sensitive information from leaking to competitors or the media. At Apple, computer engineers working on

Dressing for the Job

Most computer engineers work in a casual environment where employees dress in business casual or even T-shirts and jeans. Lax dress codes are related to the nature of the work. Computer engineers might be required to crawl under desks, lift bulky hardware, stoop, bend, reach, and perform other office acrobatics. Casual clothing is much more practical than formal office dress. The Our Everyday Life website offers some dress tips for a computer hardware engineer job: "Avoid jewelry that can get caught, or worse, cause a short to you or the hardware when bending over pieces and parts of computers. If you can't lose the necklace, at least tuck it in your shirt when troubleshooting. Neckties are also a danger for getting caught where you don't want them to, tuck them into the middle of your shirt or don't wear them if not required."

Flip-flops and shorts might also be dangerous for those working in labs or on factory floors where dangerous equipment is in operation. When working with power tools, soldering irons, and other equipment, computer engineers might be required to wear goggles, hard hats, or other safety gear.

Our Everyday Life, "How to Dress for a Computer Hardware Job," October 4, 2017. https://oureverydaylife.com.

the iPhone were sequestered in a secure, windowless room that was off limits even to the cleaning crew. Engineers could only refer to the project using the code name "Purple." As the iPhone project expanded, the company moved engineers into an entire building on its Cupertino, California, campus. They were on permanent "lockdown," as Forstall explains: "We put in doors with badge readers [and] there were cameras. I think to get to some of our labs, you had to badge in four times. . . . [And] the first rule about the Purple Project is you do not talk about that outside of those doors."[32] Like employees at other tech companies, Apple engineers signed nondisclosure agreements (NDAs). These legal documents spelled out penalties such as dismissal or monetary fines for those who disclosed sensitive information.

The integrity aspect of the CIA triad requires that data remain consistent, accurate, and trustworthy. This requires computer engineers to take steps to ensure that data cannot be deleted or altered by accident or by unauthorized sources. Availability, the third aspect of the triad, is about making sure that all data and computer equipment is accessible at all times. Secure usernames and passwords are required to access data. In terms of computer engineering, availability means having backups on external hard drives or in the cloud to restore data if necessary. Backup power supplies, redundant computers, and other equipment also ensure availability.

Brainstorming

Computer engineers perform numerous tasks while maintaining confidentiality, integrity, and availability. When projects are being developed, a computer engineer will attend many meetings with mechanical engineers, software engineers, and a chief technical officer (CTO) who oversees the technical direction of the company. Development meetings might continue for weeks or months. After a decision is made to create a new product, computer engineers will develop the documents and plans necessary to execute every step of the process from prototypes to production.

During the earliest stage a computer engineer will create what is called an architecture document. This contains all of the details about the proposed system, including which internal components will be used, how it will interface with other equipment, how much storage it will have, and how it can be expanded. During this process the computer engineer works with mechanical engineers. The team figures out details on the physical design, such as how much interior space will be available for components. The architecture document and the physical details will be sent to the software team, the production team, and others who will review the plans, offer suggestions,

> "Sometimes we'll just sit down to discuss an exciting idea that some of us might have stumbled upon and see if it might turn into something that solves one of our problems."[33]
>
> —Zeeshan Zia, computer engineer

and perform their own development work. Numerous team meetings follow. Computer engineer Zeeshan Zia, who works on self-driving cars, explains the process: "Once every few days, I'll meet colleagues to discuss progress on the sub-system we are responsible for, brainstorm new ideas if we're stuck on something. Sometimes we'll just sit down to discuss an exciting idea that some of us might have stumbled upon and see if it might turn into something that solves one of our problems."[33]

Once the basic details of a product are settled, the computer engineer will design the circuits and other hardware components. This often involves conducting research online to learn what the competitors are doing and what new technology might be available to incorporate into the product. Phone calls and e-mails are exchanged with purchasing managers who will procure components needed to build the product. However, creating a new product is not always straightforward, as computer hardware engineer Dave Haynie explains: "Part of this process is building the model of your system in your mind. In fact, over time, that's one of the more critical things. . . . I've been stuck on a problem more than once, called it a night, got in my car, put on some loud rock music, and, driving really fast on twisty roads, found that [my mind] could spit out very good suggestions about the problem."[34]

> "Part of this process is building the model of your system in your mind."[34]
>
> —Dave Haynie, computer hardware engineer

Stitching It Together

After Haynie settles on a system, he says he sits down at a powerful PC connected to several monitors and opens up a CAD (computer-aided design) software program such as Altium Designer. The software allows him to create page after page of schematic designs consisting of coordinated systems and subsystems. These designs are eventually turned into real printed circuit boards (PCBs) filled with chips, resistors, connectors, capacitors, filters, and other components. The schematic design phase can take hours, weeks, or longer if the engineer gets new ideas to incorporate or management introduces new goals or requirements.

When the system is finalized, the computer engineer uses CAD software to design a working 3D model of the product. Packing the numerous components efficiently into a case is called stitching. This can be demanding work, according to Haynie: "[Stitching is] essentially solving a big puzzle of connections between components. You define the layers in the system . . . and then it's drawing, drawing, drawing [using CAD software]. I did it for 45 straight hours [in 2014], on a tight deadline before a vacation. Good to find your limits from time to time, but not recommended too often."[35]

Interns and Conferences

In addition to the basic tasks of designing computer hardware, computer engineers work with interns, oftentimes collaborating on papers to present at conferences. Computer engineer Zeeshan Zia, who works on self-driving cars, describes this aspect of his work life:

> During summers, we get interns (usually final year PhD students), and I'll be meeting them every couple of days for a few hours, discussing results, brainstorming on a white board. Last year, I was collaborating with two, so it took 1–2 hours almost every day. Around two weeks before major conference deadlines, we will start writing papers perhaps spending a few hours every day. . . . Two to three times a year, I will visit one of the major computer vision or robotics conferences that last around a week. There I might talk to former colleagues and friends, try to get to know some new people, do a bit of tourism, as well as skim through the more interesting papers. . . . No, I don't drive around in a "self-driving" car all day though! The vast majority of my typical workdays are spent working on . . . data.

Zeeshan Zia, "What Is a Typical Day Like Working on Self-Driving Cars?," *Forbes*, February 13, 2017. www.forbes.com.

When stitching is completed, the computer engineer creates digital blueprints for the manufacture of PCBs in a 2D CAD format called Gerber. Working with a manufacturing engineer, the computer engineer creates assembly drawings and a bill of materials that will be needed to make the product. When a new product is being developed, about ten to fifteen prototypes are built. Then testing begins. Computer engineers, software engineers, and others perform numerous experiments and trials to ensure that everything works as expected. Sometimes there are mistakes that require tiny wires to be soldered under a 3D microscope. Large companies have technicians for this type of work, but computer engineers who work for start-up companies perform such tasks themselves.

Prototype testing inevitably reveals numerous glitches. Haynie describes the next step: "[You have] a whole list of problems and go back to your CAD system, make a new project from your [original] design and proceed to correct all problems, add new features, not introduce any new problems, and start the whole physical process over again. And maybe again and again. . . . At some point, there will also be actual production."[36]

A Job with Many Titles

In 2018 some of the large companies employing computer engineers include HP, Intel, Apple, and Texas Instruments. Computer engineers also work in business sectors where computer-controlled systems are needed. They build control systems and instrumentation for manufacturers and create systems architecture for major corporations. Computer engineers develop software and software architecture for computer firms, work as hardware engineers for chipmakers, and create digital systems for broadcasting. Some work to design cutting-edge medical equipment, while others are creating the first generation of artificial intelligence machines.

Depending on where they work, computer engineers hold many titles. An engineer might be referred to as field service engineer, hardware design engineer, hardware engineer, design engineer, systems integration engineer, systems engineer, senior hardware engineer, project engineer, or network engineer. As the numerous job titles demonstrate, computer engineers are flexible enough to take on many roles. But whatever the job description, computer engineers are required to perform every day at work, as Brandon R. Buckhalt explains: "An engineer gets paid to THINK."[37]

CHAPTER 5

Advancement and Other Job Opportunities

"In today's reality, engineers are the new leadership class," according to Geoffrey C. Orsak, dean of engineering at Southern Methodist University in Dallas. Orsak points to a recent article by the global executive search firm SpencerStuart that shows nearly a quarter of all CEOs running Fortune 500 companies were educated as engineers and computer scientists. While not all were computer engineers, engineering was the most common college major among these CEOs, while number two was business administration. Orsak adds, "A young college graduate with an engineering degree is approximately six times more likely than a graduate with a business degree to become a CEO of an S&P 500 corporation."[38]

> "In today's reality, engineers are the new leadership class."[38]
>
> —Geoffrey C. Orsak, dean of engineering, SMU

Whether or not a computer engineering grad eventually takes the helm at Texas Instruments or HP, that student will be earning a good salary within five years of graduation. In 2016 the median annual pay for a computer engineer was $115,080 according to the Bureau of Labor Statistics (BLS). The median salary is the wage at which half the computer engineers earn more while half earn less. The lowest-paid computer engineers earned around $66,870, while the highest paid earned more than $172,010. Several factors contribute to the difference between the highest and lowest wage earners. One difference is regional: The median wage for computer engineers in southern states like Florida was around $86,000. Computer engineers who worked in California tech capitals like San Francisco and

Entry-level computer engineers are expected to continue developing knowledge and skills even after starting their first job. And, like new employees starting in all fields, they must prove themselves to their supervisors.

Silicon Valley (around San Jose) were earning a median wage above $143,630.

Wages for computer engineers were higher in particular industries. Makers of magnetic and optical storage devices—hard disks, semiconductors, and flash drives—paid computer engineers around $132,930 in 2016. Semiconductor and electronic component manufacturers paid computer engineers an average of $133,480, while computer and peripheral equipment makers were paying around $120,000 annually.

The most lucrative field for computer engineers is being fueled by the race to develop self-driving cars. According to the employment analysis firm Paysa, the shortage of experienced computer engineers needed to perfect autonomous car technology was pushing annual salaries in Silicon Valley and San Francisco to an average of $295,000 in 2017. Google's self-driving car division Waymo was offering experienced computer engineers over $283,000 with a $30,000 signing bonus, while compensation at

Uber was higher, at $348,000. Top computer engineers who specialized in autonomous car hardware were earning as much as $405,000. Sebastian Thrun, a computer engineer who founded Google's self-driving car project, explains the high salaries: "We are at the start of an entirely new period in human history with autonomous vehicles. I expect the competition for [computer engineering] talent to continue for some time."[39]

On the other end of the pay scale, computer engineers working for the federal executive branch of the government, such as the Commerce Department, were bringing in around $108,790 in 2016. While this might seem low for computer engineers, it is well above the $41,520 average annual salary earned by all Americans that year.

A Junior Computer Engineer

The BLS figures are for computer engineers who have several years of job experience. But college grads do not generally earn the average wage when first out of school. Most begin their careers as junior engineers at an established company. According to the employment website Glassdoor, a junior computer engineer who has been certified by the Institute of Electrical and Electronics Engineers (IEEE) can earn about $75,000 annually. Those working for a major defense contractor like Northrop Grumman can expect to begin their careers earning around $85,000 a year. Junior engineers who are lucky enough to work on space programs at NASA will bring home nearly $96,000 yearly.

Wherever they work, entry-level junior computer engineers are expected to be good team players who follow orders and take direction from engineers with more experience. Junior computer engineers learn about teamwork through consultation with engineers of different disciplines. During the early phases of their career, junior engineers spend time familiarizing

"We are at the start of an entirely new period in human history with autonomous vehicles. I expect the competition for [computer engineering] talent to continue for some time."[39]

—Sebastian Thrun, computer engineer

themselves with their employer's policies and procedures. Although they are done with school, junior computer engineers are expected to continue developing their knowledge base and technical skills through self-learning. And they must prove themselves to supervisors by performing their assignments successfully and finishing ahead of schedule. These actions help them land more challenging projects.

After three to five years on the job, most junior computer engineers advance to the next level. They continue to focus on their technical specialties, but at this stage they might be appointed as team leaders for small groups of junior computer engineers or specialists. Computer engineers with five years of experience are empowered to assign roles and responsibilities to each of their team members. This type of work usually leads up the career ladder to a role as project leader. These computer engineers guide several small teams or a single large team. This type of work attracts the attention of company executives and might lead to financial bonuses and other job perks.

Mentoring Others

Computer engineers who have been on the job five to ten years often act as mentors who counsel those with less experience, called protégés. Good mentors enhance the careers of protégés by providing technical and business advice. Workplace mentors help protégés demonstrate their skills to their bosses by steering them toward challenging assignments. Mentors explain company policies, traditions, and values; share expertise; help protégés deal with setbacks and problems; and provide career coaching. Silicon Valley engineer Ilea Graedel explains the value of mentorships: "It's important for more experienced engineers to share their knowledge with younger generations. . . . It's great to have a dedicated person who is interested in passing along their knowledge and expertise. . . . It's also great when older colleagues let you know that they are available to help if you need them."[40]

After around ten years on the job, computer engineers can advance to the role of lead engineer. In this role they spend their days directing activities performed by several large teams. Lead

Other Career Options

Some computer engineers find themselves seeking new opportunities in related fields. Those who seek new employment prospects have several career options. Computer engineers have many technical skills that can be used in the aerospace industry where engineers design aircraft, satellites, missiles, and spacecraft. Aerospace engineers earn an average annual salary of $109,650.

Computer network architects build communication networks with materials such as computers, servers, routers, network drivers, cables, and software programs. In 2016 computer network architects earned an average salary of $101,201 creating local area networks (LANs), wide area networks (WANs), Internet portals, and e-mail networks for their employers.

Computer engineers with master's degrees can find work as computer and information research scientists. These professionals earn a median annual wage of $111,840 inventing and designing new approaches to computing technology. Computer and information research scientists are employed in business, medicine, science, and manufacturing.

There is a very high demand for IT managers, formally referred to as computer and information systems managers. IT managers can earn more than $135,000 annually by planning, coordinating, and directing a company's digital activities. Computer engineers can also move up to an executive position, such as a CTO who determines the overall technical direction of a company.

computer engineers are familiar with the technical objectives set out by their company's chief technical officer and other executives. As lead engineers they oversee all aspects of a project's design, testing, building, and production. They ensure projects are completed within budget and on schedule. The advanced management and leadership skills possessed by lead computer engineers help them organize teams, plan projects, set company objectives, work with customers, and solve problems. At this career level, computer engineers might also hire and fire employees and offer raises and promotions.

Computer engineers who advance to this level are often regarded as industry experts. They might hold several patents for devices or systems they invented. (A patent is a legal document that provides the holder the right to collect money from others who use the invention.)

A Fork in the Road

Computer engineers who have worked for ten to twenty years often come to a fork in the road regarding their careers. Some choose to continue working as lead computer engineers, while others move into management. Those who remain in the technical realm often take on more responsibilities. They oversee major projects and design flagship products for their company. Some experienced computer engineers publish technical papers or return to academia for advanced training and degrees.

Computer engineers who move into management need to hone new skills when taking on more business-oriented tasks. The engineers focus their talents on the overall financial well-being of their company, overseeing finances, banking, personnel, marketing, customer relations, and profit and loss. Some computer engineers moving into management return to school to obtain an MBA (master of business administration).

At this advanced career level, twenty to thirty years after graduation, computer engineers determine their company's technical approaches and supervise the entire engineering workforce. They perform many duties simultaneously, including running departments, mentoring junior engineers, updating their education and training, and developing their leadership skills. Computer engineers who are in the later stages of their careers might also wish to share their knowledge and experience through teaching, writing books, or publishing articles. Some quit their firms to start their own companies.

Moving On to Other Opportunities

It is very rare for computer engineers to spend decades at a single firm since they possess skill sets that are in high demand across the tech industry. Some experienced computer engineers get job offers from competing companies several times a year. If they are unhappy at work, or feel their company is headed in the wrong direction, computer engineers might interview with someone new just to see what is available. Google engineer John L. Miller explains the experience common to all engineers in his field: "You hear about the new [job]. Maybe from a friend, maybe from a recruiter flattering you, maybe in the trade rags. If you're good and you get as far as investigating, you're probably going to get an offer somewhere, and you're probably going to move. Who wouldn't move when offered more money to do something more interesting?"[41]

Most moves are motivated by money. According to the BLS the average annual raise for an American worker was 3 percent in 2015. But a talented computer engineer can receive a signing bonus plus a 10 percent to 50 percent pay increase when moving on to a new opportunity. Business writer Vivian Giang explains this phenomenon: "Job hoppers are believed to . . . be higher performers, and even to be more loyal, because they care about making a good impression in the short amount of time they know they'll stay with each employer."[42]

Wherever computer engineers work, they use their training to create extremely detailed plans for systems designed to function flawlessly. The same kind of detailed analysis, when applied to a career, can create a professional environment filled with opportunity. Nearly every CTO, and many tech CEOs, began their work lives as junior engineers. The road to the top might have been a winding path or a straight highway. But those who invest their time and energy in a computer engineering career can find great job satisfaction as they work their way from junior engineer to a senior-level technical expert.

CHAPTER 6

What Does the Future Hold for Computer Engineers?

When Tara Thomas was growing up in her native India, she was fascinated with the way computers worked. She began writing her own software programs in high school. As an undergraduate student, Thomas studied electrical engineering and computer science, which she says gave her a "holistic picture" of the way hardware and software work together. In 2017 Thomas was a twenty-five-year-old grad student pursuing a master's degree in computer engineering at Purdue University. Even before her spring graduation, Thomas says she "had her foot in the door of a real career"[43] as a computer engineer working on projects for General Electric and Apple.

Thomas's skills are in great demand because of the rapid rise in what is called advanced manufacturing or Industry 4.0. This booming economic sector—which includes the auto, aerospace, communications, manufacturing, and energy industries—is characterized by companies deeply involved in technology research and development (R&D). According to a study by the Brookings Institute, advanced manufacturing industries will be the most consequential and dynamic drivers of the US economy in the coming decades.

Industry 4.0 is centered on high-performance computing, computer-aided design, high-precision production technologies, advanced robotics, and computer control systems. According to tech journalist Linda Marsa, career opportunities for computer engineers include "designing high-tech hardware for the defense and aerospace industry, devising cybersecurity encryption and data protection systems, working in robotics and health care analytics, and, of course, feeding the hunger for new and better consumer electronics."[44]

Advanced manufacturing entities are clamoring for big thinkers like Thomas and other computer engineers to invent, test, and produce the cutting-edge digital technology needed to improve products and production methods. And Thomas's work reflects this need. At Apple she helped create a prototype of an easier-to-use keyboard. At General Electric she devised a new system of embedded sensors that wirelessly communicated real-time information about production bottlenecks and other problems. As Jelena Kovacevic, head of the electrical and computer engineering department at Carnegie Mellon University, says: "The supersonic pace of technological innovation is creating an unprecedented set of opportunities for these young engineers."[45] However, the supersonic pace of computer engineering is not reflected in figures compiled by the government.

> "The supersonic pace of technological innovation is creating an unprecedented set of opportunities for these young [computer] engineers."[45]
>
> —Jelena Kovacevic, electrical and computer engineering professor

The BLS says the employment outlook for computer engineers is expected to grow by only 5 percent through 2026, about as fast as the average for all occupations. Around 73,600 people worked as computer engineers in 2016, and the government predicts that number to grow to 77,600 by 2026. According to the BLS, more technological innovation is taking place in the software industry than in the computer hardware sector. However, the BLS figures mainly focus on the computer and electronic product manufacturing industry, which experienced slow growth throughout the 2010s.

Opportunities Abound

While the BLS says employment for computer engineers is expected to remain relatively flat, industry experts say the bureau is behind the times. For example, a study by the International Federation of Robotics (IFR) shows that more than 1.7 million new industrial robots will be installed in factories worldwide through

Hot Jobs in Artificial Intelligence

In 2018 *Time* magazine ran an article called "The 25 Hottest Careers Right Now." *Time* listed computer vision engineer as the third hottest job. Computer vision engineers use their knowledge of artificial intelligence (AI) to develop hardware and software used by robots in numerous industries. These professionals create vision algorithms that recognize patterns and allow robots to identify and position objects, or pick and place materials on assembly lines. Like other AI specialists, computer vision engineers are in great demand. *Time* wrote that the number of job postings for computer vision engineers grew by 169 percent between 2017 and 2018, and the average base salary was $131,297.

The year-over-year growth in job postings for all AI engineers surpassed those of all other employment sectors in 2018. The number of want ads more than doubled since 2015, and demand is expected to remain high for those who concentrate on machine learning and computer vision engineering. With companies increasingly incorporating robotics and AI into their business strategies, it is no surprise that computer engineers who specialize in artificial intelligence will be capitalizing on this accelerating tech trend well into the future.

2020. These robots are part of a trend where industries are building "smart factories" that rely on machine learning and artificial intelligence. Robots in numerous smart factories will be linked together in the cloud. They will use machine learning techniques to "teach" each other new ways to optimize their efficiency. Computer engineers will be working to design, program, and customize these machines for food processing, assembly, resource extraction, and other tasks. In addition to creating full-time work for computer engineers, the robotics industry will require an increasing number of freelance engineers who will act as consultants, systems designers, and repair personnel.

There is also a "wild upswing" in companies hiring computer engineers who specialize in virtual reality (VR) and AI, according to Paysa CEO Chris Bolte: "We see this type of engineer as one of the hottest engineers out there. These far-reaching categories that are shaping the future of things, that's where companies are putting major investments." Bolte adds, "The competition for these people, it's pretty outstanding, which is why you see such big salaries."[46]

According to the website Road to VR, demand for job candidates with VR knowledge is expected to grow 37 percent a year for the foreseeable future. And companies like Google, Oculus, and Samsung were having a hard time meeting demand in 2018. Much of VR hardware development is rooted in PC and smartphone technologies, which means most computer engineers can transfer their skills. Nate Beatty, cofounder of IrisVR, asserts that "the virtual reality space is taking off, and I believe the job opportunities are only going to grow in the next few years. . . . Anyone who can pick up new tech easily . . . and is forward-thinking . . . would be a prime candidate for lots of awesome new B2B (business-to-business) VR startups."[47]

Companies need computer hardware engineers who can design smaller VR headsets, increase performance and optical quality, and improve battery and connectivity. While VR gaming start-ups in Silicon Valley are providing multiple opportunities, numerous other industries have plans to enter the VR market. Architecture, engineering, and construction firms are working to incorporate VR equipment into 3D design processes. Medical, defense, and educational entities are planning to use VR for simulations and training purposes. Computer engineers will be central to these new developments and will also play roles in project management, support and business development, and as CTOs and CEOs.

A Different Model

While the VR and robotics industries are accelerating at a rapid pace, demand for computer engineers is sure to be high in a business that is still in its infancy. The quantum computing industry is expected to move business, science, and government forward in unprecedented ways.

Quantum computers can solve problems in seconds that would take traditional computers years. As Goldman Sachs tech researcher Toshiya Hari says, "Quantum computing isn't just your classic computer on steroids. It is a completely different model."[48]

According to a 2018 study Hari conducted for Goldman Sachs, the quantum computer industry will be worth $37 billion by 2021. And while computer giants like Google and Intel are investing huge sums of money in quantum computing, there is a shortage of computer engineers who have the experience necessary to work in the field. As David Reilly, director of Microsoft Quantum Laboratories explains: "We need a new type of [computer] engineer. One part deep mathematician with a grasp of quantum physics; one part motor mechanic, capable of creating entirely new devices as we encode and manipulate information at the level of single electrons or photons of light."[49]

> "We need a new type of [computer] engineer. One part deep mathematician with a grasp of quantum physics; one part motor mechanic, capable of creating entirely new devices."[49]
>
> —David Reilly, director, Microsoft Quantum Laboratories

Prospective computer engineers who envision a future where they are in high demand and paid high wages have many places they can apply their talents. While the PC and smartphone markets might be slowing, demand is soaring for computer engineers who want to pursue a cutting-edge career in quantum computing, virtual reality, or robotics. While the tech world continues to change, those who wish to change the world will find no shortage of opportunities if they hold a degree in computer engineering.

CHAPTER 7

Interview with a Computer Engineer

Azhar Zuberi has been a computer engineer since the late 1990s. After a stint as senior engineering manager for Intuit/TurboTax, Zuberi cofounded the start-up Contentlinq.com, a Software as a Service (SaaS). He has been the chief technical officer of Contentlinq.com since 2014.

Q: Why did you become a computer engineer?

A: In college I majored in physics and astronomy with an emphasis on software engineering (which was an unusual mix at the time). I got an internship to work at a submillimeter telescope facility (JCMT) on top of Mauna Kea in Hawaii, which exposed me to computer engineering. At that time the web was still in a nascent stage, and I immediately saw how computers would soon become an integral part of everyday life. I became really interested in human/computer interactions—from the hardware level to user interfaces.

Q: Can you describe your typical workday?

A: At the telescope, my job was primarily working with senior instrumentation engineers and scientists. The telescope sat at close to 14,000 feet (4,267 meters) above sea level in harsh conditions and would often go out of focus. This frustrated visiting astronomers. My job was to work with the team and build a holography system that would keep the telescope in focus in real time. My typical workday would involve writing firmware (which is a low-level form of software) to control a data acquisition system.

Most of my time was spent in the lab writing code and debugging. During release periods we would go to the summit to deploy and test the latest features.

Q: What do you like most about your job?

A: You really have to push your boundaries every day to solve unique problems as they arise. You have to get really creative and often have to invent solutions on the fly. I also like working with large multidiscipline teams and learning from others. I am able to bring a lot of this acquired discipline into other areas of my life—like playing music with others.

Q: What do you like least about your job?

A: It is important for people considering going into the field to be mindful of maintaining a work-life balance. It is really easy, especially for young people, to get knee deep in a complex project and lose sense of time—sometimes for days on end. This could potentially lead to a very unhealthy existence (both mentally and physically) and quick burnout.

Q: What personal qualities do you find most valuable for this type of engineering work?

A: Creativity, ability to think analytically (like a computer), patience, ability to work with large multidisciplinary teams and diverse personalities. The ability to learn quickly, as technology changes at the speed of light.

Q: What is the best way a student can prepare for this type of engineering job?

A: Start learning to code as soon as possible. Learn about different hardware architectures, programming languages, compilers, and debugging tools. Look for something around the house you think could be better through automation, and try to build a solution. The hardware and software tools available nowadays are cheap and easy to get up and running with.

Q: What other advice do you have for students who might be interested in a career as a computer engineer?

A: I was fortunate that my university offered a co-op program that placed students in real-life work environments during alternating semesters. Due to this, in addition to the telescope gig, I got a chance to spend some time studying acoustics for the National Research Council of Canada. I also got a chance to work at the Stanford Linear Accelerator Center (SLAC), which is a high-energy physics lab/particle accelerator. This gave me a lot of diverse exposure to the types of jobs computer engineers do. As a result I was able to hit the ground running once I left school. So the advice is to try and get exposure to as many different areas of computer engineering while still in school—and perhaps look for schools that have a co-op/internship program.

SOURCE NOTES

Introduction: Engineers Make It Work

1. Quoted in Patrick Thibodeau, "Steve Wozniak: Engineering Matters," *Computerworld*, October 8, 2014. www.computerworld.com.
2. Quoted in Thibodeau, "Steve Wozniak."
3. Quoted in Meg Murphy, "Building the Hardware for the Next Generation of Artificial Intelligence," *MIT News*, November 30, 2017. http://news.mit.edu.
4. Quoted in John Boudreau, "Q&A with Apple Co-Founder Steve Wozniak," *Seattle Times*, April 10, 2006. www.seattletimes.com.

Chapter 1: What Does a Computer Engineer Do?

5. Quoted in Quora, "Is a Computer Engineer Able to Design Computer Hardware like Motherboards, CPUs, GPUs, and Graphics Cards, or Is This the Job of Electrical Engineers?," May 7, 2017. www.quora.com.
6. Quoted in Quora, "Is a Computer Engineer Able to Design Computer Hardware like Motherboards, CPUs, GPUs, and Graphics Cards, or Is This the Job of Electrical Engineers?"
7. Daniel Burrus, "The Internet of Things Is Far Bigger than Anyone Realizes," *Wired*, November 2014. www.wired.com.
8. Quoted in Alan Ohnsman, "Autonomous Car Race Creates $400K Engineering Job for Top Silicon Valley Talent," *Forbes*, May 27, 2017. www.forbes.com.
9. Quoted in Rich Rovito, "Rethink Robotics," *BizTimes*, February 19, 2018. www.biztimes.com.
10. Quoted in Aaron Frank, "Machines Teaching Each Other Could Be the Biggest Exponential Trend in AI," SingularityHub, January 21, 2018. https://singularityhub.com.
11. Quoted in David Pring-Mill, "Everyone Is Talking About AI—but Do They Mean the Same Thing?," SingularityHub, March 15, 2018. https://singularityhub.com.
12. Quoted in Murphy, "Building the Hardware for the Next Generation of Artificial Intelligence."
13. Quoted in Andrew J. Hawkins, "Elon Musk Thinks Humans Need to Become Cyborgs or Risk Irrelevance," *Verge*, February 13, 2017. www.theverge.com.

Chapter 2: How Do You Become a Computer Engineer?

14. Quoted in CareerVillage.org, "What Types of Classes Can I Take While in High School to Prepare for a Computer Science Degree in College?," October 23, 2015. www.careervillage.org.

15. Quoted in CareerVillage.org, "What Types of Classes Can I Take While in High School to Prepare for a Computer Science Degree in College?"

16. Quoted in *Princeton Review*, "Systems Analyst," www.princetonreview.com.

17. Quoted in Ki Mae Heussner, "How to Pick the Best MOOCs: 6 Tips from a Coursera Junkie," Gigaom, August 9, 2013. https://gigaom.com.

18. Quoted in Quora, "What Is Computer Engineering and How Difficult Is the Major?," May 28, 2016. www.quora.com.

19. Tracy Chou, "What Are the Advantages and Disadvantages, and Short and Long Term Financial/Career Implications, of Doing a Computer Science PhD?," Quora, October 1, 2014. www.quora.com.

20. Chou, "What Are the Advantages and Disadvantages, and Short and Long Term Financial/Career Implications, of Doing a Computer Science PhD?"

21. Quoted in *U.S. News & World Report*, "What Is a Computer Network Architect?," 2018. https://money.usnews.com.

Chapter 3: What Skills and Personal Qualities Matter Most—and Why?

22. Brandon R. Buckhalt, "About," Creative Engineer, 2018. www.thecreativeengineer.com.

23. Quoted in Buckhalt, "About."

24. Quoted in Quora, "What Skills Should a Computer Engineering Student Have?," April 14, 2015. www.quora.com.

25. Alison Doyle, "Essential Skills You Need to Become a Top Engineer," Balance Careers, January 30, 2018. www.thebalance.com.

26. Quoted in Mark Crawford, "How Engineers Can Improve Technical Writing," ASME, September 2012. www.asme.org.

27. Quoted in Lindsay Tigar, "7 Indispensable Soft Skills to Develop for 2018," Ladders, December 12, 2017. www.theladders.com.

28. 3DX, "7 Skills Needed to Be a Top Engineer," *3DxBlog*, July 10, 2015. http://blog.3dconnexion.com.

29. Quoted in Tigar, "7 Indispensable Soft Skills to Develop for 2018."

30. Joseph Stiglitz, "In No One We Trust," *Opinionator* (blog), *New York Times*, December 21, 2013. https://opinionator.blogs.nytimes.com.

Chapter 4: What Is It like to Work as a Computer Engineer?

31. Quoted in Brian Merchant, "The Secret Origin Story of the iPhone," *Verge*, June 13, 2017. www.theverge.com.

32. Quoted in Merchant, "The Secret Origin Story of the iPhone."

33. Zeeshan Zia, "What Is a Typical Day Like Working on Self-Driving Cars?," *Forbes*, February 13, 2017. www.forbes.com.

34. Quoted in Quora, "What Do You Do in a Day as a Computer Hardware Engineer?," August 12, 2016. www.quora.com.

35. Quoted in Quora, "What Do You Do in a Day as a Computer Hardware Engineer?"

36. Quoted in Quora, "What Do You Do in a Day as a Computer Hardware Engineer?"

37. Buckhalt, "About."

Chapter 5: Advancement and Other Job Opportunities

38. Quoted in Brandon R. Buckhalt, "A Few Common Myths About Engineers," Creative Engineer, 2018. www.thecreativeengineer.com.

39. Quoted in Ohnsman, "Autonomous Car Race Creates $400K Engineering Job for Top Silicon Valley Talent."

40. Quoted in Gary McCormick, "Monkey See, Monkey Do: The Benefits of a Mechanical-Engineering Mentorship," *Redshift*, February 29, 2016. www.autodesk.com.

41. John L. Miller, "Why Do Software Engineers Change Jobs So Frequently?," *Forbes*, February 6, 2018. www.forbes.com.

42. Vivian Giang, "You Should Plan on Switching Jobs Every Three Years for the Rest of Your Life," *Fast Company*, January 7, 2016. www.fastcompany.com.

Chapter 6: What Does the Future Hold for Computer Engineers?

43. Quoted in Linda Marsa, "Opportunities Abound for Those Studying Engineering," *U.S. News & World Report*, March 17, 2017. www.usnews.com.

44. Marsa, "Opportunities Abound for Those Studying Engineering."

45. Quoted in Marsa, "Opportunities Abound for Those Studying Engineering."

46. Quoted in Ohnsman, "Autonomous Car Race Creates $400K Engineering Job for Top Silicon Valley Talent."

47. Quoted in Caroline Zaayer Kaufman, "How to Land a Job in Virtual Reality Tech," Monster, 2018. www.monster.com.

48. Toshiya Hari, "Quantum Computers: Solving Problems in Minutes, Not Millennia," Goldman Sachs, February 2018. www.goldmansachs.com.

49. Quoted in Michael Bailey, "'Part Physicist, Part Motor Mechanic': Quantum Computer Engineer Shortage Threatens Hub Hopes," Financial Review, March 12, 2018. www.afr.com.

Accreditation Board for Engineering and Technology (ABET)

415 N. Charles St.
Baltimore, MD 21201
www.abet.org

ABET accredits college and university programs in engineering and engineering technology at the associate, bachelor's, and master's degree levels. ABET accreditation provides assurance that a college or university program meets the quality standards of the profession for which that program prepares graduates. The organization's website provides lists of ABET-accredited programs, information about attaining accreditation, and links to information about workshops and scholarships.

Association for Computing Machinery (ACM)

2 Penn Plaza
New York, NY 10121
www.acm.org

The ACM is the major educational and scientific society for educators and engineers. The website offers cutting-edge publications, books, blogs, research papers, and career resources. The education section features a digital library, a learning center, and numerous resources beneficial to K–12 students through those earning a doctorate degree.

Black Girls Code (BGC)

PO Box 640926
San Francisco, CA 94164
www.blackgirlscode.com

The goal of the BGC is to train one million girls of color to code by the year 2040 and to become the "Girl Scouts of technology." The organization hosts hackathons, workshops, and other events for girls ages twelve through seventeen.

Codecademy

49 W. Twenty-Seventh St.
New York, NY 10001
www.codecademy.com

This online school offers free coding lessons in numerous programming languages, including Git, AngularJS, JavaScript, and CSS. Students can sign up and begin coding within minutes.

iD Tech

910 E. Hamilton Ave.
Campbell, CA 95008
www.idtech.com

iD Tech partners with over 150 top colleges and universities to provide computer summer camp programs for students ages seven through seventeen. An all-girls program is offered to students ages ten through fifteen. Campers can learn AI, build computers, code video games, and participate in other digital activities.

IEEE Computer Society

2001 L St. NW
Washington, DC 20036
www.computer.org

The IEEE is dedicated to computer science and technology. The society publishes numerous journals, provides networking and career development resources, and sponsors more than two hundred technical conferences annually. The student activities section of the website is a comprehensive resource for those interested in a career in computer engineering.

INDEX

ABOUT THE AUTHOR

Stuart A. Kallen is the author of more than 350 nonfiction books for children and young adults. He has written on topics ranging from the theory of relativity to the art of electronic dance music. In 2018 Kallen was named "Green Earth Book Award" winner for his book *Trashing the Planet: Examining Our Global Garbage Glut*. In his spare time, Kallen is a singer, songwriter, and guitarist in San Diego.